The DECLARATION of INDEPENDENCE

In CONGRESS, July 4, 1776.

The unanimous Declaration of the thirteen united States of America.

When in the Course of human events, it becomes necessary for one people to dissolve the political bands which have connected them with another, and to assume among the powers of the earth, the separate and equal station to which the Laws of Nature and of Nature's God entitle them, a decent respect to the opinions of mankind requires that they should declare the causes which impel them to the separation.

We hold these truths to be self-evident, that all men are created equal, that they are endowed by their Creator with certain unalienable Rights, that among these are Life, Liberty and the pursuit of Happiness.

[The remainder of the document consists of the body of the Declaration and the signatures of the signers, including John Hancock, Button Gwinnett, Lyman Hall, Geo Walton, Samuel Chase, Wm Paca, Thos Stone, Benjamin Rush, Benjamin Franklin, John Morton, Josiah Bartlett, Wm Whipple, Saml Adams, John Adams, Robt Treat Paine, Step Hopkins, William Ellery, Roger Sherman, and others.]

documents of
DEMOCRACY

The DECLARATION *of* INDEPENDENCE

by stephen krensky

MARSHALL CAVENDISH BENCHMARK
NEW YORK

With thanks to Catherine McGlone,
a lawyer with a special interest in constitutional law and American history,
for her legal eagle eye in perusing the manuscript

Copyright © 2012 Stephen Krensky
Published by Marshall Cavendish Benchmark An imprint of Marshall Cavendish Corporation

Other Marshall Cavendish Offices:
Marshall Cavendish International (Asia) Private Limited, 1 New Industrial Road, Singapore 536196
• Marshall Cavendish International (Thailand) Co Ltd. 253 Asoke, 12th Flr, Sukhumvit 21 Road,
Klongtoey Nua, Wattana, Bangkok 10110, Thailand • Marshall Cavendish (Malaysia) Sdn Bhd, Times
Subang, Lot 46, Subang Hi-Tech Industrial Park, Batu Tiga, 40000 Shah Alam, Selangor Darul
Ehsan, Malaysia

LIBRARY OF CONGRESS CATALOGING-IN-PUBLICATION DATA
Krensky, Stephen. The Declaration of Independence / by Stephen Krensky. p. cm. — (Documents
of democracy) Includes bibliographical references and index. ISBN 978-0-7614-4913-3 —
ISBN 978-1-60870-670-9 (ebook) 1. United States. Declaration of Independence—Juvenile
literature. 2. United States—Politics and government—1775-1783—Juvenile literature. I. Title
E221.K74 2012 973.3'13—dc22 2010023649

Editor: Joyce Stanton   Art Director: Anahid Hamparian
Publisher: Michelle Bisson   Series Designer: Michael Nelson

Photo research by Linda Sykes Picture Research, Inc., Hilton Head, SC
The photographs in this book are used by permission and through the courtesy of:

©iStockphoto: cover; The Granger Collection: 1, 6, 8, 10, 13, 17, 18, 21, 24, 29, 31, 34, 38, 43, 50, 54,
57, 65; The National Archives: 2; Bettmann/Corbis: 6; Musee Carnavalet, Paris/The Bridgeman Art
Library: 62; The Library of Congress: 67; Hisham Ibrahim/Photodisc/Getty Images: 73.

Printed in Malaysia (T)
135642

Half-title page: Thomas Jefferson and members of his committee present their draft of
the Declaration to the Second Continental Congress in Philadelphia, June 1776,
in a painting by John Trumbull.
Title page: The Declaration of Independence

Contents

A Call *for* Liberty

The temperature in Philadelphia on July 2, 1776—a comfortable 72°F—was unusual for midsummer. But there was nothing comfortable about the mood in the State House on Chestnut Street. After almost two months of meeting in large groups and small committees, more than fifty delegates from the thirteen British colonies had gathered for an announcement. This Second Continental Congress, as the group was called, had argued and analyzed the rights and wrongs of their relationship with Great Britain. Much had been discussed, and no point left untouched.

For more than ten years, the American colonists had asked their king, George III, for relief from unfair taxes—and they had been refused. They had asked for

Above: June 28, 1776. Thomas Jefferson and his fellow committee members present their draft of the Declaration to the Second Continental Congress. This picture is a detail from the famous painting by John Trumbull that hangs in the Capitol in Washington, D.C. See page one of this book for the full image.

representation in the British Parliament to air their views—and they had been refused that, too. Their relationship had frayed to the point where the colonists had begun an armed rebellion—and still their complaints had not been taken seriously.

The delegates had disagreed about many things already, and they would disagree again in the future. But for now, they had reached a consensus. They were done being bullied. It was time to part company with their English king, a misguided ruler who treated them as little more than wayward children.

Did the colonies really have a chance to break free of Great Britain, a country whose armed forces dwarfed their own? Or were they embarking on a fool's quest? Even the most angry and radical delegates didn't know for sure. But everyone's feelings and ideas stood out clearly in the document that lay before them, their declaration of independence.

As president of the Continental Congress, John Hancock of Massachusetts spoke up a few weeks later while signing the final draft. "We must be unanimous," he commented. "There must be no pulling different ways. We must all hang together." Legend has it that another delegate, Benjamin Franklin of Pennsylvania, added a line of his own. "We must all hang together," he tartly observed, "or assuredly we shall all hang separately."

The port of Philadelphia in the late 1700s

Chapter One

Welcome *to the* New World

THE ROOTS OF THE DECLARATION OF Independence stretched back over many years, but even they had their limits. Civic unrest and dissatisfaction had not always marked life in Britain's American colonies. Until the first half of the 1700s, settlers were too busy staking claims to the New World to worry about the pros and cons of their relationship with England.

Most of the colonies had been founded in the 1600s. Virginia had led the way with the first permanent settlement at Jamestown in 1607. Eleven other colonies had followed rather quickly, the last being Pennsylvania in 1682. The lone exception was Georgia, a relative newcomer dating only to 1733.

Since these were British colonies, they were largely settled by British men, women, and children. And when these hopeful emigrants sailed across the Atlantic, their allegiances were not magically transformed. They had been British citizens before they left port from Liverpool or Southampton, and they remained British

Quakers, guided by their simple but profound religious faith, settled in Pennsylvania in the 1600s.

citizens upon their arrival in Boston, New York, Philadelphia, or Norfolk. Even after they adjusted to their new surroundings, they all still looked to England for their customs, their education, and their protection.

Not that their aim was simply to create another England on the far side of the Atlantic. Some, like the Quakers of Pennsylvania and the Puritans of Massachusetts, were seeking a religious freedom that England had refused to provide. Some were seeking a fresh start for personal or financial reasons. Still others were lured by the prospect of adventure, of facing the unknown.

But whatever their circumstances and motives, the new colonists were not aiming to cut themselves off from their past. The Pilgrims may have felt most unwelcome in England, but they moved to "New" England after all, and borrowed most of their local place names from home. Early settlers to Virginia may have been drawn by the lure of rich farmland, but they still sent many of their sons back to England to be properly educated.

Admittedly, a few frustrations and problems had cropped up. British law, for example, prohibited finished goods from being produced in the colonies. Iron mined in Massachusetts was sent to England to be turned into nails. Beavers hunted on the American frontier had their furs cut, shaped, and sewn by London tailors before being sold as coats or hats in European markets.

This was more than just inconvenient for the colonists. It was a loss of revenue and industry. Even worse, all that manufacturing, handling, and shipping forced the colonists to pay a much higher price for finished goods than they would have paid if such things were made closer to home. And of course, much time was wasted with all the movement back and forth. In the mid–1700s, the fastest Atlantic crossings took two months, and ships only made the voyage a few times a year. So placing an order and then waiting for it to be filled was a time-consuming process.

And when the ordered goods did finally make an appearance, they were not always what had been requested. British merchants took advantage of the distance from their colonial customers to get rid of overstock in their inventory or to pass off a lesser-quality product for a higher-priced one. A wealthy planter from Virginia named George Washington was known to complain that his orders from England often arrived late and sometimes did not include the actual items he wanted, but instead contained inferior substitutes. This was an outrage. But nobody in authority seemed to care. And from three thousand miles away, there wasn't much Mr. Washington or any other colonist could do to protest.

Still, if consumer dissatisfaction had been the only issue to arise, the colonists might have shrugged it off. But more problems were coming to the surface. For decades the English and the French had been at odds trying to divide up eastern North America. The American Indian tribes, whose legitimate claim to the land was conveniently ignored by both European powers, were caught between them. Some tribes allied themselves with the English while others made pacts with the French. Major battles were fought mostly on the frontier, but smaller skirmishes were a constant danger in many other places as well.

THE HIGH COST OF PEACE

In 1763 the Treaty of Paris between Great Britain and France brought an end to the last of the French and Indian Wars. After seven years of fighting, Great Britain had finally won, and as a result, the French forever lost their claims to Canada and the Ohio Valley. It was a severe blow to their power and influence.

The British naturally applauded this outcome, but their victory had not come cheap. The war had been dreadfully expensive, and with the coming of peace, there were bills to be paid. Since the end of the hostilities would benefit the colonies directly, the British government in London thought it only fitting that they pick up much of the cost.

The head of that government was King George III. At twenty-five, he was a relatively new monarch, having inherited the throne only three years before. As kings went, George III was pretty unassuming. He liked plain food and comfortable clothes. His interest in music, architecture, and science was genuine and thoughtful. Most unusual of all for a king, he was happily married to his wife of two years, Queen Charlotte, with whom he would eventually have fifteen children.

King George III, determined to be strong and resolute

George III was stubborn, though. He thought his grandfather and great-grandfather (Georges I and II) had relinquished too much power to Parliament. This had made them look weak or, at least, uninterested. George III was determined to be neither. He wanted to show everyone that he was a strong and resolute ruler. Unfortunately, in the case of the American colonies, he chose at least some wrong things to be strong and resolute about.

His ministers soon implemented a string of acts—the Stamp Act, the Navigation Acts, the Townsend Acts, the Intolerable Acts, and more—all designed in one way or another to raise money from the colonies. These measures irritated the colonists, and the more legislative tricks the British tried, the angrier the colonists became. Many of these acts were soon repealed, but "No taxation without representation" became a popular rallying cry because the colonists had no voting representatives in Parliament, where all the acts were passed.

Underscoring the ongoing tensions was one simple fact. The British government and the colonists no longer shared the same view of colonial lands. For Britain, the colonies were something to be developed and exploited to the advantage of the mother country. It had been that way from the beginning, and nothing had changed. The colonists saw things differently. By the 1760s, their population topped 1,600,000. Many of these people were not English emigrants. They had been born and raised in the colonies. America was their true home, and their lives were something very distinct and separate from those of their English ancestors.

THE POLITICAL GAP WIDENS

Two such opposing views could not peacefully coexist for long. By the 1770s, patience was running thin on both sides. Boston was the headquarters for the hotter heads among the angry colonists. John Hancock, the cousins Sam and John Adams, and others were all members of the Sons of Liberty, an informal group of men who were publicly unhappy with British rule and made speeches protesting the British government's actions. Sam Adams was a struggling businessman and John Adams a lawyer still making a name for himself. But John Hancock was one of the wealthiest men in the colonies, and despite the risk of losing his money if condemned as a traitor, he was among the earliest of those calling for freedom from England.

When a new tax on tea was imposed, it was angry Bostonians who reacted most dramatically. On December 16, 1773, a band of men masquerading as Indians boarded three merchant ships in Boston Harbor and dumped their cargo of tea overboard. It was an act that became and remains famous as the Boston Tea Party. But their exhilaration was short-lived. The British government reacted with a harsh penalty. The Port of Boston was closed, causing widespread economic distress. Of course, it also had the result of embittering the colonists even more.

Opposing British rule, however, was not the same as wishing for independence. That was a drastic step, the kind most sensible people were not even considering. True, the colonists had serious grievances, but they were still loyal British subjects. Even Sam Adams, who deferred to no one in his indignation over the treatment of the colonies, was still insisting in 1774 that "the restoration of union and harmony between Great Britain and the colonies" was a goal "most ardently desired by all good men."

Such hopes, however, were dealt a severe blow the following spring. Following the closure of the port, tensions had continued to mount in Boston. Hoping to further cripple the colonials' confidence, General Thomas Gage, the British commander in Boston, decided to act. He sent an armed force to the town of Concord, about twenty miles away, to capture an armory of colonial ammunition and weapons.

On the night of April 18, 1775, seven hundred red-coated British soldiers secretly marched out from Boston. But thanks to the work of several men, including a silversmith named Paul Revere, word of the British advance was revealed. The fighting, which began early on April 19 in Lexington and continued on a much larger scale in Concord later in the day, did not go well for the British. By nightfall, the redcoats were retreating to Boston. Close to three hundred of them were either wounded or killed along the way.

MORE THAN JUST FIGHTING WORDS

Three weeks after the Battle of Lexington and Concord, the Second Continental Congress met in Philadelphia. These delegates from twelve of the thirteen colonies (Georgia declined at first to send any repre-

In the early-morning light of April 19, 1775, "the shot heard round the world" was fired on Lexington Green.

sentatives) were the successors to the First Continental Congress, which had met the previous fall. That body had appointed itself to represent colonial interests, and since no one had protested that claim, the job had become theirs. The First Continental Congress had presented a united front, declaring their rights and publishing a petition of their grievances against British actions. They hoped that speaking in one voice would increase their chances of being heard. But King George III wasn't listening.

Many members from the First Continental Congress had returned for the gathering of the Second. Still, while they had agreed to meet, the delegates were hardly unanimous in their views. Southern colonies worried about

A VARIED GROUP
OF DELEGATES

The Second Continental Congress was convened on May 10, 1775. That date had been designated as one of the final acts of the First Continental Congress the previous fall. It was chosen in the event that King George III did not act favorably on the petition stating the colonists' grievances. When the king acted as expected—denouncing the petition—the call went out for the delegates to assemble.

The states picked their delegates according to their own wishes, and the majority had served in the earlier Congress. They were all local leaders elected

Above: The back of Independence Hall, Philadelphia, some twenty years after the delegates met there

either by their colonial assemblies or by the provincial congresses that had sprung up after some of the royal governors appointed by England had dissolved the existing legislatures. Many of the delegates did not favor independence, though they all recognized that the situation was dire. Most had been born in the colonies, but there was no rule about this. It turned out that one delegate was originally from Wales, two from England, two from Scotland, and three from Ireland. None of them were professional soldiers eager to start a war. They were mostly merchants and lawyers, doctors and farmers. At the age of seventy, Benjamin Franklin was the oldest. The youngest was twenty-four-year-old James Madison of Virginia. But whatever their personal or professional backgrounds, they were all intent on resolving the thorny issues before them.

Not all of the delegates had yet arrived when Congress opened on May 10, but given the issues at hand, it was decided to start without them. Peyton Randolph of Virginia, who had served as president of the First Continental Congress, was again chosen to lead the Second. But when illness forced him to return home, John Hancock took his place as president. As for the Virginia delegation, it now sent for Thomas Jefferson, a most fortunate development considering the key role Jefferson was soon to assume.

agriculture, while northern colonies worried about the growth of cities. Smaller colonies feared being pushed around by bigger ones. Bigger colonies worried that smaller colonies would have more influence than they should.

For all their differences, though, the delegates were agreed on one thing: enough was enough. Following the fighting at Lexington and Concord, colonial militias from all around New England had moved to surround Boston. On June 15, Congress appointed George Washington as the commander in chief of this Continental army.

GENERAL WASHINGTON TAKES COMMAND

It had been decided that a Virginian would have the best chance of holding the respect of both northern and southern colonies, and Washington was certainly that. But he was not necessarily the obvious choice. At forty-three, he lacked the education of his fellow leaders. He had not attended college, and he was far happier holding a riding crop in his hand than holding a book. After marrying the wealthy widow Martha Custis in 1759, he had devoted himself to his family (Martha had two young children from her first marriage) and developing his plantation, Mount Vernon.

Still, Washington had a certain way about him, a stature that went beyond his imposing height of six foot two. In one backwoods battle during the 1750s,

Washington conveyed an aura of courage and fortitude that seemed to make him a natural commander.

two horses had been shot out from under him and four bullets had pierced his coat—all leaving him unharmed. "I heard the bullets whistle," he wrote afterward, "and, believe me, there is something charming in the sound."

While accepting his commission, Washington was well aware that he had no experience with conventional warfare. He expressed to Congress his belief that he was not equal to the task. Still, he did not shrink from his duty. On July 3, 1775, in Cambridge, Massachusetts, he took charge of about 16,000 men from various colonies. Although his new soldiers shared a desire for freedom, they had different habits, customs, and accents. So they didn't always get along. At one point, for example, after several months of too little food and supplies, a full-fledged brawl broke out among hundreds of men. Suddenly, General Washington appeared on horseback. According to one excited young observer, the general "leaped from his saddle . . . and rushed into the thickest of the melee, with an iron grip seized two tall, brawny, athletic, savage-looking riflemen by the throat, keeping them at arm's length, alternating shaking and talking to them." As onlookers gathered around, Washington's display of raw strength and fearlessness quickly ended the fight.

"I heard the bullets whistle, and, believe me, there is something charming in the sound."

—George Washington

No such easy resolution was in sight with Great Britain. Many colonists had supposed that once they raised a large united force, the British would show the wisdom to seek some sort of compromise. But this was not to be. Nevertheless, Congress proclaimed that, despite the fact that it had supported the creation of a new army, it did not mean to break away from Great Britain. Benjamin Franklin and John Adams even headed a mission to meet secretly in New York with the British commander Lord Richard Howe. However, Howe was only authorized to return things to the way they had been before the fighting had begun, perhaps with an amnesty for the rebellious leaders. There would be no acknowledgment of the colonial grievances, no attempt to iron them out. This was completely unacceptable to Franklin and Adams. How could the British continue to be so blind? In polite but profound disappointment, they left New York as quickly as they had come.

THE PUSH FOR INDEPENDENCE

Several more months of fighting only hardened the positions of everyone involved. So did the publication in January 1776 of an anonymous pamphlet (later credited to writer Thomas Paine) called *Common Sense*. Paine had done some writing previously, but nothing that matched the significance of this latest effort. He held a very dim view of monarchies, especially the British one. He took particular pleasure in skewering the virtues of hereditary

THOMAS PAINE

Thomas Paine was born in Thetford, England, in 1737. As a boy, he was apprenticed to his father as a corset maker. Later, he ran away to sea. At twenty-three, he lost his first wife and child in childbirth not long after the failure of his first business. Subsequent jobs as tax collector and teacher did not go well, either, although it was during this time that he did his first political writing. In 1774 he had the good fortune to meet Benjamin Franklin. That same year, Paine came to America, and he carried with him a letter of introduction to Franklin's son-in-law, Richard Bache.

Two years after his arrival in the colonies, Paine published his influential pamphlet *Common Sense*. He began by examining the basic fabric of civilization:

> Some writers have so confounded society with government, as to leave little or no distinction between them; whereas they are not only different, but have different origins. Society is produced by our wants, and government by our wickedness; the former promotes our happiness

Above: Thomas Paine, two years before his death in 1809

positively by uniting our affections, the latter negatively by restraining our vices. . . . Society in every state is a blessing, but government even in its best state is but a necessary evil; in its worst state an intolerable one.

And what of the long-standing relationship between Great Britain and America? Paine was quick to dismiss it. "I have heard it asserted by some," he wrote, "that as America hath flourished under her former connection with Great Britain, that the same connection is necessary towards her future happiness, and will always have the same effect. Nothing can be more fallacious than this kind of argument. We may as well assert, that because a child has thrived upon milk, that it is never to have meat."

Paine later wrote another important work, *Rights of Man*, which had great influence during the French Revolution. But his success and influence did not provide him with an easier life. After moving to France in 1790, he was imprisoned when his enemies came to power, and he later condemned French emperor Napoléon Bonaparte for his dictatorial ways. Paine returned to the United States in 1802, but it was not a popular homecoming. He had publicly feuded with George Washington, and many of his ideas were now out of favor. When he died seven years later, a few people noticed, but hardly anyone seemed to care.

privilege. Paine wrote that among English kings the bad ones far outnumbered the good ones. He also questioned the assumption that government was inherently a good thing. Rather, he saw it as a necessary evil that protected human beings from the worst parts of themselves.

Paine also maintained that America mattered to England only so far as it served the purposes of the British Empire. He viewed this as a one-way and unacceptable position. He concluded that the only logical course was to make a declaration of independence as soon as possible.

What had once seemed to be a dream or a fit of madness, depending on the loyalties involved, was fast becoming very real. *Common Sense* sold over 150,000 copies at a time when book sales of 1,000 were respectable. Paine had managed to find the words for what a great many people were already thinking. Further momentum was provided by the fighting already taking place. As for George III, he had obviously made up his mind, having declared that the war of these rebels was clearly designed with the aim of creating a new empire.

The king's words may have been premature when they were uttered in the fall of 1775. Seven months later, after further battles in Massachusetts as well as Virginia, North Carolina, and South Carolina, they looked rather different. In May 1776, members of Congress passed a resolution avowing the colonies' right to form their own local governments. It was partly composed by John Adams, who wrote the preamble. He described his experience in a letter to his wife, Abigail, with whom he engaged in frequent correspondence. (Their marriage was an unusual intellectual partnership for the time, and Abigail never hesitated to speak her mind, nor would her husband have wanted it any other way.) "Great Britain," John wrote to Abigail, "has at last driven America to the last step, a complete separation from her; a total, absolute independence, not only of her Parliament, but of her crown."

On June 7, Richard Henry Lee, a delegate from Virginia, introduced to his fellow members of Congress several statements that became known as the Lee Resolution. One was that "these United Colonies are, and of right ought to be, free and independent States." The second, a partner to the first, was "that all political connection between them and the State of Great Britain is, and ought to be, totally dissolved."

Lee's supporters insisted that such a formal and unequivocal assertion of independence was necessary for public morale and to impress upon foreign powers that the British colonists in America were deadly serious in their intentions. Thus far, the rest of the world had not looked on the fourteen months of fighting as a war between nations. To the world, Great Britain was facing only a domestic uprising. It was troubling and messy to deal with, but none of anyone else's business.

The vote on the Lee Resolution was postponed for

three weeks because a number of the delegates, including those from Maryland, Pennsylvania, Delaware, New York, and New Jersey, were not authorized by their governments to vote for independence. During this period, supporters of the resolution worked to convince those colonial governments to vote for it. At the same time, a committee was appointed to draft a formal declaration, so that it would be ready when independence, which almost everyone recognized was now inevitable, was approved. Its members were scientist and printer Benjamin Franklin of Pennsylvania and four lawyers: Roger Sherman of Connecticut, Robert R. Livingston of New York, John Adams of Massachusetts, and Thomas Jefferson of Virginia.

At thirty-three, Jefferson was the youngest and also the least known of the group. His father, Peter, was a well-to-do planter with little in the way of a formal education or manners. His mother, the former Jane Randolph, came from one of Virginia's most distinguished families. So Jefferson had seen both the aristocratic and yeomen worlds up close. He had come to dislike the British model of hereditary rule, in which kings and nobles led society simply through a lucky accident of birth. He wanted people to be judged by their abilities, not their pedigrees, which was convenient in his case since his own talents were considerable. Jefferson was also known for being evenhanded and calm in his dealings with other people, but it would have

Thomas Jefferson lived in this house in Philadelphia when he worked on the Declaration of Independence.

been a mistake to underestimate his steely resolve. As he would write in a letter eleven years later, "The tree of liberty must be refreshed from time to time with the blood of patriots and tyrants."

Long afterward, John Adams stated that Jefferson's reputation as a fine writer (two years earlier he had penned a series of resolutions called *A Summary View of the Rights of British America*) was one factor in his being chosen to write the Declaration. But there were others. Franklin was too ill, Adams was from Massachusetts (home of the most radical elements in Congress), and neither Sherman nor Livingston put himself forward. As a Virginian, Jefferson represented the most populous colony, and one thought to be the most balanced in its sentiments.

The full committee met several times, probably at Franklin's home in Philadelphia because he was suffering from gout and other ailments that made traveling difficult. They continued to discuss the ideas that the Declaration should include, but left the specific wording to Jefferson.

Jefferson titled his first draft "A Declaration by the Representatives of the United States of America, in General Congress assembled." (It would continue to be called that until July 19, 1776, when Congress, in voting to have the Declaration printed on parchment, directed it to be called "The unanimous Declaration of the thirteen united States of America.") He composed it between June 11 and June 28, rising early each day to scribble on a portable writing box he had designed himself. He wrote the document in sections, leaving space between the lines for amendments. He did not expect to get it right the first time through. After marking the paper with changes and corrections, he would copy the text over to start again cleanly.

Both Franklin and Adams saw rough versions of the document, but they suggested only a few changes. On June 28, the committee reported back to Congress. Before considering the text of the document, Congress had to vote on the Lee Resolution—whether to vote for or against independence. Not everyone was convinced of the proper action to take. Independence opponents worried that countries such as France and Spain would see the Declaration as a threat, fearing that it would lead to further uprisings in their own colonies. But those delegates in favor brushed aside

A Declaration by the Representatives of the UNITED STATES OF AMERICA, in General Congress assembled.

When in the course of human events it becomes necessary for one people to dissolve the political bands which have connected them with another, and to assume among the powers of the earth the separate and equal station to which the laws of nature & of nature's god entitle them, a decent respect to the opinions of mankind requires that they should declare the causes which impel them to the separation.

We hold these truths to be self-evident, that all men are created equal, that they are endowed by their creator with equal & inherent & inalienable rights, that among these are life, & liberty, & the pursuit of happiness; that to secure these ends, governments are instituted among men, deriving their just powers from the consent of the governed; that whenever any form of government shall becomes destructive of these ends, it is the right of the people to alter or to abolish it, & to institute new government, laying it's foundation on such principles & organising it's powers in such form, as to them shall seem most likely to effect their safety & happiness. prudence indeed will dictate that governments long established should not be changed for light & transient causes: and accordingly all experience hath shewn that mankind are more disposed to suffer while evils are sufferable than to right themselves by abolishing the forms to which they are accustomed. but when a long train of abuses & usurpations [begun at a distinguished period & pursuing invariably the same object, evinces a design to subject reduce them under absolute despotism,] it is their right, it is their duty, to throw off such government & to provide new guards for their future security. such has been the patient sufferance of these colonies; & such is now the necessity which constrains them to expunge their former systems of government. the history of the present king of Great Britain is a history of unremitting injuries and usurpations, [among which appears no solitary fact to contradict the uniform tenor of the rest all of which have] in direct object the establishment of an absolute tyranny over these states. to prove this, let facts be submitted to a candid world, [for the truth of which we pledge a faith yet unsullied by falsehood.]

The first page of Thomas Jefferson's rough draft, with amendments suggested in part by Benjamin Franklin and John Adams

such concerns. In their view, Congress needed the formal statement in order to proclaim its authority to negotiate with foreign powers.

THE POINT OF NO RETURN

On July 1, Congress gathered for further debate. At least one delegate, John Dickinson of Pennsylvania, was alarmed at how angry the Lee Resolution appeared. He was concerned, and rightly so, that such a document would bury any chance for reconciliation with Great Britain. Six or even three months earlier, his views would have found a more sympathetic audience. Now most of the other delegates simply wanted to press ahead.

An unofficial vote was taken later in the day. Nine colonies stood in favor of independence. Of the other four, Pennsylvania and Delaware were divided, South Carolina was opposed, and New York was unable to vote until authorized by its colonial government. A formal vote was delayed for a day in the hope that the reluctant delegates could be brought around. And indeed they mostly were. When the vote was taken on July 2, the colonies were unanimous except for the New York delegates, who still had to abstain, having not yet received further instructions from home. (Those instructions, giving them permission to vote for independence, would come the following week.) The text of the Declaration was finally approved by Congress on July 4 and sent off to be printed.

Again, John Adams reported the events of the day to his wife:

> Yesterday the greatest Question was decided, which ever was debated in America, and a greater perhaps, never was or will be decided among Men. A Resolution was passed without one dissenting Colony "that these united Colonies, are, and of right ought to be free and independent States, and as such, they have, and of Right ought to have full Power to make War, conclude Peace, establish Commerce, and to do all the other Acts and Things, which other States may rightfully do." . . . When I look back to the Year 1761, and recollect the Argument . . . which I have hitherto considered the Commencement of the Controversy, between Great Britain and America, and run through the whole Period from that Time to this, and recollect the series of political Events, the Chain of Causes and Effects, I am surprized at the Suddenness, as well as the Greatness of this Revolution.

The recent events may have seemed "sudden" to Adams because, although colonial frustrations had been building for many years, in the course of just a few months, a major decision had been taken—one from which there could be no turning back.

For Jefferson, the Declaration first and foremost had to be "an expression of the American mind."

Chapter Two

A Formidable Juggling Act

IN BEGINNING THE DRAFT OF A suitable declaration, Thomas Jefferson faced four significant challenges. One, he had to find a way to encapsulate the philosophy that made independence a justifiable demand. Two, he had to list the shared grievances that had already brought the colonies to a state of war with Great Britain. And three, he had to voice these sentiments in words that all the colonies would support, no small feat considering the differing perspectives the colonies represented.

The fourth challenge was meeting the short deadline Congress had set. On June 10, the five-man committee was charged with creating a document. The committee was to report back to Congress eighteen days later. So Jefferson, whatever his preferences might have been, did not have the option of composing his thoughts at leisure. He had to write fast.

To be sure, Jefferson was not starting from scratch. Several existing documents provided a foundation for his ideas—including philosopher John Locke's 1690 *Second Treatise on Government*, the First Continental Congress's Declaration of Rights and Grievances from 1774, the Second Continental Congress's Declaration of the Causes and Necessities of Taking Up Arms (which Jefferson himself had cowritten in 1775), and the Virginia Declaration of Rights, written just the month before. Jefferson never claimed, either at the time or at any point during the rest of his famous life, that his thoughts were original. As he wrote many years later in reflection, "Whether I had gathered my ideas from reading or reflection I do not know. I know only that I turned to neither book nor pamphlet while writing it. I did not consider it as any part of my charge to invent new ideas altogether."

> *"Whether I had gathered my ideas from reading or reflection I do not know. I know only that I turned to neither book nor pamphlet while writing it. I did not consider it as any part of my charge to invent new ideas altogether."*
>
> —*Thomas Jefferson*

Considering the time constraints alone, it is not surprising that Jefferson chose to tread on familiar ground. As he described his thought process in composing the Declaration: "Neither aiming at originality of principle or sentiment, nor yet copied from any particular and previous writing, it was intended to be an expression of the

American mind, and to give to that expression the proper tone and spirit called for by the occasion. All its authority rests then on the harmonizing sentiments of the day."

This makes a lot of sense. For any document to gain the necessary support from the delegates and later the public, the ideas would have to be ones that they were comfortable with already. New and controversial notions would not have been welcome. Something strong yet familiar could stir a patriotic heart. Something unfamiliar might lead to puzzled expressions and the scratching of heads.

So what was the final result? To begin with, the Declaration has four distinct sections. The first is the preamble, or introduction, which sets forth the reason for writing it. The second outlines the civic philosophy that the colonies believed governed their actions. The third is the list of charges, or grievances, that the colonies held against King George III. And the fourth is the Declaration itself, which Congress presented as the natural and inevitable consequence of the other three sections.

THE PREAMBLE

The first sentence, which makes up the entire introduction, is as follows:

> When in the Course of human events, it becomes necessary for one people to dissolve the political bands which have connected them with

TRACING THE WORDS OF LIBERTY

George Mason (1725-1792) was a Virginia planter who was active in politics. At the request of the Virginia Convention of Delegates, he wrote the Virginia Declaration of Rights in  the weeks before Jefferson started writing the Declaration of Independence. It was published on June 12, 1776, just as Jefferson was beginning his work. It stated that "all men are by nature equally free and independent, and have certain inherent rights . . . namely, the enjoyment of life and liberty, with the means of acquiring and possessing property, and pursuing and obtaining happiness and safety."

Clearly, the key phrases "enjoyment of life and liberty" and "pursuing and obtaining happiness" have counterparts in the Declaration. But these similarities of phrase do not mean that Jefferson borrowed his words directly from Mason. They do, however, confirm the notion that such ideas were already at large among the political men of the time.

Noteworthy also is Jefferson's omission of the reference to property. The Declaration's elegant, simple phrase "the pursuit of happiness" reflected his own broader view of a philosophical ideal.

Above: George Mason, principal author of the Virginia Declaration of Rights

another, and to assume among the powers of the earth, the separate and equal station to which the Laws of Nature and of Nature's God entitle them, a decent respect to the opinions of mankind requires that they should declare the causes which impel them to the separation.

Here at the outset, Jefferson made two bold claims at once. He presented the colonies and Great Britain as equals who had previously entered into a partnership. This interpretation must have come as news to the British, who looked on the colonies as essentially belonging to them. A fundamental tenet of the period held that colonies were a captive extension of the countries that founded them. They properly served as a source of raw materials and a ready market for manufactured goods. Under Jefferson's new definition of the relationship, if one partner believed the other side was not holding up its end, then the partnership, the "political bands," could and should be dissolved.

In the Declaration of Rights and Grievances published by the First Continental Congress in 1774, the focus had been on the colonists' rights as Englishmen. In that document, the colonists claimed that those rights were being denied and they were simply seeking justice from their government. But a lot had happened in two years. Jefferson was no longer seeking the colonists' rights as Englishmen but was instead making a bold new claim. He was declaring that all men had natural human rights, and if their government violated them, they had the right to break free.

Merely stating these sentiments was not the same as getting everyone to accept them. The colonies were challenging the right of kings to rule as they pleased. But how could they justify this action? The only possible defense was to turn to a higher authority than a king—in this case the laws of nature and the idea of God.

And to strengthen the impression that Congress and the colonists were courtly people embarking on a diplomatic quest, Jefferson made sure to note that they were concerned about the "opinions of mankind." It would be ungentlemanly, and perhaps disrespectful of history, to simply proceed without justifying their actions. The members of Congress were not mere rabble-rousers; they were educated men of principle. Therefore it made sense to be polite about explaining, as the Declaration dryly put it, "the causes which impel them to the separation."

WHERE SHOULD A GOVERNMENT COME FROM?

The second section of the Declaration begins with its most famous line: "We hold these truths to be self-evident, that all men are created equal, that they are endowed by their Creator with certain unalienable Rights, that among these are Life, Liberty and the pursuit of Happiness."

As Jefferson later wrote, he may not have consciously borrowed from earlier sources when working on the Declaration, but he had a good memory and he wasn't shy about using it. And while he chose his words carefully, some changes were made along the way. For example, "We hold these truths to be self-evident" was a suggestion from Franklin to replace "We hold these truths to be sacred and undeniable." And "among these are Life, Liberty and the pursuit of Happiness" was formerly "among which are the preservation of life and liberty and the pursuit of happiness." Such changes may seem small taken individually, but together they sharpened the power of the text.

The first paragraph of this section continues:

> That to secure these rights, Governments are instituted among Men, deriving their just powers from the consent of the governed, — That whenever any Form of Government becomes destructive of these ends, it is the Right of the People to alter or to abolish it, and to institute new Government, laying its foundation on such principles and organizing its powers in such form, as to them shall seem most likely to effect their Safety and Happiness. Prudence, indeed, will dictate that Governments long established should not be changed for light and transient causes; and accordingly all experience

hath shewn, that mankind are more disposed to suffer, while evils are sufferable, than to right themselves by abolishing the forms to which they are accustomed.

Jefferson presented as an accepted fact that people start with natural rights. This was not an assumption that everyone necessarily shared, though it was a current view among many eighteenth-century writers and philosophers. Jefferson stated this not because it was popular, but because it was the foundation for all his other points. In order to maintain their natural rights, people create governments. If any government fails in its responsibility, then it is more than the right, it is the obligation of the people under that government to remove it and install another. As Jefferson noted in the Declaration, human nature is more likely to endure "evils" if they are "sufferable," that is, not too oppressive. But at whatever point the evils become insufferable, the government must be overthrown.

It is commonly thought that the philosopher John Locke, particularly in his *Second Treatise of Government* of 1690, was a strong influence on Jefferson. Locke had ideas that influenced many other thinkers of the eighteenth century, including the European philosophers Voltaire, Jean-Jacques Rousseau, and Immanuel Kant. Locke believed that people were born with an empty mind that would be shaped by their experi-

"Every man has a property in his own person. This nobody has a right to, but himself."—John Locke

ences. He defended the role of government in society, but he also held that any government was accountable to the people it served.

As Locke had written, a governed people retained the right to remove their government should it act contrary to their trust. In his case, Locke was writing about the English Revolution of 1688, which had removed the Catholic king James II from the throne and replaced him with his nephew, the Dutch Protestant William of Orange-Nassau, who became William III.

Locke's situation was similar to Jefferson's in that both men were trying to justify the overthrow of a king. As the Declaration made clear: "When a long train of abuses and usurpations, pursuing invariably the same Object evinces a design to reduce them under absolute Despotism, it is their right, it is their Duty, to throw off such Government, and to provide new Guards for their future security. — Such has been the patient sufferance of these Colonies; and such is now the necessity which constrains them to alter their former Systems of Government."

In granting that people had the right to dissolve an unjust government, Jefferson was deliberately not specific about what form an effective new government might take. It might seem logical for him to champion a democracy or republic, governments created by the people themselves. But this would have been an insult to the monarchs of western Europe, none of whom ruled by election. Jefferson was not trying to present a picture of opposition to any and all monarchies. At least on the surface, the Declaration was no threat to a good and wise king.

Why was Jefferson careful not to offend any European monarchies? Well, the revolution would cost money. Congress was planning to seek financial and military support from the European powers, all of which were led by royalty. Offending them would not be a good first step in that direction. So the colonists took pains to make it clear that they were rebelling against King George III not simply because he was a king, but because as a king he had not treated his subjects with the justice that all people deserve.

RAILING AGAINST THE KING

The Declaration's third section underscored the king's failings by itemizing the "history of repeated injuries and usurpations, all having in direct object the establishment of an absolute Tyranny over these States. To prove this, let Facts be submitted to a candid world." Here Jefferson had the advantage of having practiced his points. Not long before, he had written out twenty charges against George III in connection with the preparation of a Virginia state constitution. He had accused the king of, among other things, vetoing helpful laws, obstructing immigration, approving the quartering of troops in peacetime, cutting off or limiting trade with other parts of the world, and most significantly, imposing taxes without the colonists' input or consent.

Since these conditions had not changed, Jefferson was free to use most of his charges again in the Declaration—and he did. In effect, the complaints included every injustice the colonists had suffered in the past ten or more years. In addition, since the fighting had begun the year before, the king was now also guilty of suspending legislatures, declaring war, ravaging coasts, and burning towns. His cruelty, the Declaration dramatically insisted, was "totally unworthy [of] the Head of a civilized nation."

Jefferson listed more than two dozen complaints as proof that the king had failed in a test of leadership. He then explained that every effort had been made to prompt the king to address these concerns, but that all such efforts had failed. As the Declaration stated, "In every stage of these Oppressions We have Petitioned for Redress in the most humble terms: Our repeated Petitions have been answered only by repeated injury. A Prince, whose Character is thus marked by every act which may define a Tyrant, is unfit to be the ruler of a free people."

> "A Prince, whose character is thus marked by every act which may define a Tyrant, is unfit to be the ruler of a free people."
>
> —The Declaration of Independence

Even as strong a revolutionist as John Adams thought the word "tyrant" was harsh, but Jefferson wanted to make a dramatic point. And George III, as the ultimate authority for his government, one who could not be replaced by vote or appointment (unlike, say, a prime minister), was the legitimate target for all of the colonists' frustrations.

Not that Jefferson entirely ignored the British people. The colonists had duly alerted them to the nefarious actions of their government: "We have appealed to their native justice and magnanimity, and we have conjured them by the ties of our common kindred to disavow these usurpations, which would inevitably interrupt our connections and correspondence." But having received no satisfactory response, at least not from anyone in charge, war was the only remaining option.

THE END OF THE BEGINNING

All of which led to the Declaration's conclusion. Here the announcement was made that:

> these United Colonies are, and of Right ought to be Free and Independent States, that they are Absolved from all Allegiance to the British Crown, and that all political connection between them and the State of Great Britain, is and ought to be totally dissolved; and that as Free and Independent States, they have full Power to levy War, conclude Peace, contract Alliances, establish Commerce, and to do all other Acts and Things which Independent States may of right do. — And for the support of this Declaration, with a firm reliance on the

protection of Divine Providence, we mutually pledge to each other our Lives, our Fortunes and our sacred Honor.

This last paragraph was doing more than tying up loose ends. From a practical standpoint, the purpose of the Declaration was to legitimize the colonies' quest for independence in the eyes of the world. Achieving this status would enable Congress to make treaties and operate in diplomatic channels. It was critical for other countries to accept the colonies as free and independent states, particularly such longtime British rivals as France and Spain, which might decide to lend their support. It was also important that Congress be accepted as the sole voice of the colonies. In theory, one or more other groups could have come forward claiming to speak for their fellow colonists. But none did.

The finished Declaration underwent further changes in the few days after Congress received it on June 28. These changes fell into two categories: the first were changes that Congress made in order to make the document acceptable to as many delegates as possible; the second were changes adopted to improve what they hoped would be the document's reception abroad.

As far as the delegates were concerned, the clause about slavery was perhaps the most controversial. Jefferson had originally written that King George III had "waged cruel war against human Nature itself, violating its most sacred Rights of Life and Liberty in the Persons of a distant People who never offended him, captivating and carrying them into Slavery in another Hemisphere, or to incur miserable Death, in their Transportation thither." He added that the king was "determined to keep open a Market where Men should be bought and sold. . . . He has prostituted his Negative for Suppressing every legislative Attempt to prohibit or to restrain an execrable Commerce."

Nobody actually believed that the slave trade was the king's doing. Technically, he might have sanctioned the business by allowing it to continue, but slavery was a thriving affair long before George III ever took the throne. And if he and the British government profited by it, they had many willing partners in the colonies among merchants, ship captains, landowners, and slave traders who collectively profited even more.

Some of those profiting from slavery had renounced the practice or at least were bashful about admitting their involvement. But others, notably in the colonies of South Carolina and Georgia, were unrepentant about their involvement. Jefferson himself, for all of his high-minded words, owned a number of slaves, as did many other delegates. In any event, Congress knew that such a clause was so divisive it might doom the whole Declaration to failure. And so it was removed.

THE QUESTION OF SLAVERY

Slavery was introduced into Britain's American colonies in the mid–1600s and was firmly established within fifty years. It was legally formalized in such documents as the Virginia Slave Codes of 1705. Although later banned in certain northern colonies, it remained inextricably woven into the fabric of colonial society. The slavery question was one that haunted the Declaration from the very beginning. On one side, opponents found the trade immoral and reprehensible. On the other were the proponents who had grown used to slavery's eco-

Above: George Washington on his Mount Vernon estate, speaking with his enslaved field hands

nomic advantages and wanted the naysayers to mind their own business. Several state and local economies could not survive without it, at least not without major upheavals. And this they were unwilling to endure.

Although Jefferson originally included a provision against slavery in his draft of the Declaration, it was dropped in the proceedings that followed. Jefferson commented on the loss of the slavery provision "in complaisance to South Carolina and Georgia, who had never attempted to restrain the importation of slaves and who on the contrary still wished to continue it. Our northern brethren also I believe felt a little tender under those censures; for tho' their people have very few slaves themselves yet they [have] been pretty considerable carriers of them to others." This comment was a reference to one of the routes of the Triangle Trade, in which slaves from West Africa were brought to the West Indies, where they were traded or sold for sugar, which was then carried to New England and turned into rum. The rum in turn made its way to West Africa, where it was traded for slaves—and so continued the cycle.

The Founding Fathers were concerned that trying to eliminate slavery at the time of the Declaration would tear apart the fragile union among the colonies. However, choosing to remove the issue from the Declaration hardly made it go away.

Other changes were smaller, reflecting shadings of language more than differences in political thought. For example, "inherent & inalienable Rights" was changed to "certain unalienable Rights." The very last line received an insert. The earlier version, "And for the support of this declaration, we mutually pledge to each other our Lives, our Fortunes, and our sacred Honor" became "And for the support of this Declaration, with a firm reliance on the protection of divine Providence, we mutually pledge to each other our Lives, our Fortunes and our sacred Honor." Again, the members of Congress were both cautious and nervous enough to make sure God was on their side.

"We might have been a free and great people together."

— A line deleted from Jefferson's original document

In all, the delegates made eighty-six changes and eliminated 480 words, and Jefferson was not particularly happy about any of the revisions. He sat in silence during the debate over his words, but his feelings were not in doubt. One deleted passage reflected his personal belief that the colonists must put aside their former regard for the English but not without considerable regret. "We might," he wrote poignantly, "have been a free and great people together."

The cuts were meant to focus the criticism, to keep the claims linked as strongly as possible to the idea of natural rights and liberties. The delegates took pains to make sure the Declaration painted a very particular picture of themselves. They were not trying to be impartial, to acknowledge their own responsibility for how events had reached this juncture. Nor were they merely tired of King George III or greedy for a larger piece of some local economic pie. All they wanted was what they believed every person was entitled to—rights the British had denied them in the past, were denying them in the present, and appeared to have every intention of denying them in the future—unless, that is, they did something about it.

The big announcement—the Declaration is proclaimed throughout the land.

AMERI
CA,
INDE
PEND
ANT.
1776.

Chapter Three

The News Travels Far and Wide

FIRST AND FOREMOST, THE ANNOUNCE-ment of the Declaration was big news throughout the American colonies. It was published in newspapers, announced in churches, and discussed in every tavern. Everyone was well aware, of course, that the fighting had already begun, having commenced more than a year earlier. But a true declaration of independence still created a sensation.

John Adams, for one, was ecstatic over the reaction. There was no question in his mind that this was a historic moment, a moment when, as he wrote referring to the colonies, "Thirteen clocks were made to strike as one." He also believed that July 2, the day the delegates voted for independence, would be celebrated from then on with "Games, Sports, Guns, Bells, Bonfires and Illuminations from one End of the Continent to the other." Adams was right about the celebrations but a bit less prophetic regarding the date. The final copy of the Declaration, dating from August 2, 1776, carried this bold headline: "in CONGRESS, July 4, 1776. The unanimous Declaration of the thirteen united States of America." With July 4 cited so prominently at the top of the document, the date ended up claiming a distinction it did not otherwise deserve.

Although the Declaration's specific words and phrases would be examined and analyzed in time, it was the idea of officially declaring independence that first drew everyone's attention. There was no longer any doubt about the direction Congress was taking the colonies. Many people who had held back their opinions were now roused to defend their country, even at the risk of their lives.

When the cheers subsided, everyone's attention turned to what would come next. Certainly, the fighting was bound to get more intense. "I am well aware of the Toil and Blood and Treasure, that it will cost Us to maintain this Declaration, and support and defend these States," John Adams wrote to Abigail. "Yet through all the Gloom I can see the Rays of ravishing Light and Glory."

> *"I am well aware of the Toil and Blood and Treasure, that it will cost Us to maintain this Declaration . . . . Yet through all the Gloom I can see the Rays of ravishing Light and Glory."*
> —John Adams

John Adams was a fervent patriot from the early days of the struggle.

The Declaration also had the effect of flushing out British sympathizers, who had privately hoped that things would settle down again. (Those who continued to support the British were known as Tories and, not surprisingly, they were less than popular with their fellow countrymen. Some were threatened with physical harm or damage to their property.)

Even those who did not side with the British had mixed feelings about unfolding events. They understood the need for the break with Great Britain, but they deeply regretted that such a drastic action had proved necessary. Robert Morris, a Philadelphia financier and member of Congress from Pennsylvania, wrote to a friend in New York, expressing how sorry he was that so many of his countrymen could see no way for relations with Great Britain ever to be repaired.

FROWNS AND SMILES FROM ABROAD

On the other side of the Atlantic Ocean, the reaction was understandably different. King George III was furious. How dare any of his subjects—loyal or not—defy him in this manner? In a speech, he declared:

> So daring and desperate is the Spirit of those Leaders, whose Object has always been Dominion and Power, that they have now openly renounced all Allegiance to the Crown, and all political Connection with this Country. . . . If their Treason be suffered to take Root, much Mischief must grow from it.

But not everyone in England struck such a dramatic tone. Some spoke more in sorrow than anger. The Marquis of Rockingham pointed out that the colonies had only declared their independence after they had been made to feel like enemies first.

There were also those who took issue with the Declaration on more specific terms. Some English critics found it absurd that the Declaration described the colonies as a separate people. They could see how convenient this designation was, but that didn't make it true. It had only been a year since the rebels were seeking to redress their grievances as Englishmen. Wouldn't a separate people have taken a different tack from the beginning? As for many of the charges against King George III, such as creating "a multitude of New Offices" or "quartering large bodies of armed troops" to maintain public safety, surely these were actions to be expected of any responsible king.

Further abroad, the reaction was not so much negative as cautious. No country lined up at once to be the colonies' new friend. Great Britain was the most powerful country in the Western world. If it quashed the rebellion in short order, anyone who had taken the other side might find things a bit awkward diplomatically. The French people, however, were noticeably enthusiastic about the Declaration. Still smarting from their great defeat in 1763, they were in favor of anything that gave England a bloody nose. On a more philosophical level, they also supported the Declaration's tone and content.

Such sentiments made France a logical place for Congress to turn for help. The delegates of Congress had given themselves the authority to act for the country (admittedly, there wasn't anyone else who could grant them that authority) and they intended to use it. Silas Deane of Connecticut, who could make the claim of being America's first foreign diplomat, was already in France to unofficially begin negotiations. Now two other representatives—Benjamin Franklin and Arthur Lee, a brother of Richard Henry Lee—were dispatched to join him. France finally agreed to support the American effort following the major British defeat at Saratoga, New York, in 1777. That support truly raised the possibility of an eventual American victory. Aside from the French financial loans, the addition of French ships to the war effort would prove critical. During the final battle of the war, the Battle of Yorktown in 1781, a fleet of French ships prevented a British army led by Lord Cornwallis from retreating by sea. Had British ships been able to rescue their soldiers, the war would have gone on much longer and perhaps ended differently.

MORE LASTING RAMIFICATIONS

Once the American Revolution was over and victory had been achieved, the parts of the Declaration itemizing the grievances against King George III were consigned to their place in history. They were old news, and whether truthful or invented, they weren't really worth any further debate.

Of the two most significant ramifications of the Declaration, one was intended and the other was not. Clearly, the Founding Fathers hoped that their viewpoint concerning the relationship between a government and its people would inspire others in the future. This of course turned out to include themselves, since the Declaration was a source for the later U.S. Constitution and its first ten amendments, commonly known as the Bill of Rights. While the Constitution created the government of the new nation, the Bill of Rights protected the liberties of its individual citizens. The first amendment, for example, states that "Congress shall make no law . . . abridging the freedom of speech, or of the press; or the right of the people peaceably to assemble, and to petition the Government for a redress of grievances."

It also must have been gratifying to the Founding Fathers that only thirteen years later, in 1789, the French Revolution was founded on many of the same ideals as Jefferson's famous document. Its echoes are clearly heard in the French Declaration of the Rights of Man and of the Citizen, the manifesto of their revolution. Prominent among the phrases in the French Declaration is one stating that the goal "of all political association is the preservation of the natural and imprescriptible rights of man. These rights are liberty, property, security, and resistance of oppression." Admittedly, the French revolutionaries got a lot more violent over the next few years as one faction bloodily beheaded another, but their hearts if not their heads were in the right place.

THE FRENCH
COME THROUGH

The role of France in the American Revolution spawned one of the great ironies of the late eighteenth century. On the one hand, the French were able to avenge some of their losses in the last French and Indian War by enabling the feisty American colonists to win their independence, thereby depriving Great Britain of immensely valuable lands and revenue in the future. On the

Above: The storming of the formidable prison called the Bastille on July 14, 1789, marked the violent opening of the French Revolution.

other hand, outside of the colonies themselves, the ideas put forth in the Declaration took root nowhere else as firmly as they did in France.

There were several reasons for this. The French treasury had been depleted by many wars, including the American Revolution, which had been an expensive effort to support. As famine and hardship spread across France in the 1780s, the king and his nobles showed no particular interest in correcting the situation and continued the lavish lifestyle they had embraced for so long. Ineffective financial planning and poor harvests only made matters worse. The population was ripe for change, and the ideas contained in the Declaration found a ready audience among the peasants and workers.

It must have been especially galling to King Louis XVI to think that supporting those rebel Americans years earlier contributed so greatly to his own downfall. Or maybe he never saw the connection. Either way, the results were painful as both he and his queen, Marie Antoinette, were beheaded in 1793.

In the 1800s, the principles proclaimed in the Declaration of Independence found their way to various people in Latin America and Europe. A prominent Mexican newspaper, *Semanario Político, Económico y Literario*, reprinted the entire text in 1821 as part of an attempt to raise awareness of its ideals (which were to be discussed at an upcoming Mexican Congress). The uprisings that swept across much of Europe in 1848 also looked back at the values and philosophy the Declaration espoused.

RAISING QUESTIONS OF RACIAL AND GENDER EQUALITY

Of all its influences, the words in the Declaration that continued to have the most impact were contained in the simple phrase "all men are created equal." It was not clear, though, how those words would resonate down through the years, not only for what they said, but for what they didn't say.

The first instance of their impact came immediately, for if all men were created equal, what did that mean for the fate of black men? As Thomas Hutchinson, the former royal governor of Massachusetts, tartly observed, it was hard to respect a government and a people who proclaimed that all men were created equal while holding by his count more than 100,000 slaves.

Congress had sidestepped the issue of slavery in the Declaration, leaving behind a moral time bomb that was bound to go off one day. Meanwhile, as the new states formalized their governments, it was immediately clear that the controversy was continuing. Many of the northern states put "free and equal" into their constitutions to indicate men of any color. Southern states, on the other hand, used the term "freemen" in their constitutions. And since slaves by definition weren't freemen, this left them out of the fold. (Not that the choice of words or labels was going to settle the matter.) Later, in the first half of the nineteenth century, abolitionists would continue to cite the Declaration to challenge slavery's lawful existence.

And what of women? The question of whether or not all men were created equal left women out of the picture entirely. In a letter of March 31, 1776, when John Adams was planning for the approaching congressional gathering in May, Abigail Adams had admonished him to "remember, all Men would be tyrants if they could. If perticular care and attention is not paid to the laidies we are determined to foment a Rebelion, and will not hold ourselves bound by any Laws in which we have no voice, or Representation."

Abigail Adams, intelligent, competent, and devoted wife to John, seems to have been an equal partner in their marriage.

Whatever John Adams may have privately wished, the ladies were nowhere to be found in the Declaration. And the passing decades would only increase their frustration. One woman who decided to do something about the status of women was Elizabeth Cady. Born in 1815, she took an early interest in the abolitionist movement. She was well aware from her own experiences of the rights women were denied. When she married Henry Brewster Stanton, she insisted that their vows reflect their equal stake in the relationship. In July 1848, she joined with other feminists, including Lucretia Mott and Amelia Bloomer, at the nation's first woman's rights convention, in Seneca Falls, New York. The attendees created the Declaration of Sentiments, a document that deliberately echoed the opening of the Declaration of Independence. It began:

> When, in the course of human events, it becomes necessary for one portion of the family of man to assume among the people of the earth a position different from that which they have hitherto occupied, but one to which the laws of nature and of nature's God entitle them, a decent respect to the opinions of mankind requires that they should declare the causes that impel them to such a course.

AMELIA BLOOMER

Amelia Jenks Bloomer (1818–1894) was not yet a well-known suffragette when she attended the woman's rights convention in Seneca Falls, New York, in 1848. But that would soon change. Although she had only a modest education, Bloomer started a publication in 1849 called *The Lily* to further her views on temperance, which opposed the drinking of alcoholic beverages. Later, she also propounded the idea of women's rights. One practical issue that she addressed concerned women's clothing. The fashion of the time featured dresses worn over restrictive whalebone corsets and uncomfortable hooplike bustles. Bloomer was not the  first to protest these designs, but she was among the most fervent in her objections. "The costume of women," she wrote, "should be suited to her wants and necessities. It should conduce at once to her health, comfort, and usefulness; and, while it should not fail also to conduce to her personal adornment, it should make that end of secondary importance."

Bloomer later championed a more comfortable garment featuring billowy trousers gathered at the ankles. So great was her support for the style that the pants were linked with her name and became known as bloomers. Originally from upstate New York, Bloomer soon moved to Iowa, where she remained an advocate for women's rights for the rest of her life.

Above: "The Bloomer Costume," from an old print

We hold these truths to be self-evident: that all men and women are created equal; that they are endowed by their Creator with certain inalienable rights; that among these are life, liberty, and the pursuit of happiness; that to secure these rights governments are instituted, deriving their just powers from the consent of the governed. Whenever any form of government becomes destructive of these ends, it is the right of those who suffer from it to refuse allegiance to it, and to insist upon the institution of a new government, laying its foundation on such principles, and organizing its powers in such form, as to them shall seem most likely to effect their safety and happiness.

It would take another seventy-two years before American women received the right to vote, and even today they are still fighting for equal status in other areas. But this declaration of women's rights provided the initial momentum toward achieving that end.

SLAVERY REMAINS AN ISSUE

The issue of slavery continued to face similar hurdles. It was, of course, one of the reasons for the Civil War, which began in 1861. In the Gettysburg Address of 1863, President Abraham Lincoln began by saying,

"Four score and seven years ago our fathers brought forth on this continent a new nation, conceived in liberty and dedicated to the proposition that all men are created equal." After the end of the Civil War, the Thirteenth Amendment to the U.S. Constitution was supposed to do away with slavery. It reads, "Neither slavery nor involuntary servitude, except as a punishment for crime whereof the party shall have been duly convicted, shall exist within the United States, or any place subject to their jurisdiction." However, certain states found ways around the amendment, enabling them to continue supporting the inequities that existed. And the later "separate but equal" doctrine upheld by the U.S. Supreme Court mockingly echoed Jefferson's words. In the case of *Plessy v. Ferguson* (1896), the Supreme Court upheld the right of a railroad company to designate specific areas of a train "whites only." Almost sixty more years would pass before the Supreme Court finally threw out the separate but equal doctrine in the case of *Brown v. Board of Education* (1954). Here the Court ruled that state laws creating separate public schools for black and white students actually did not give black children equal educational opportunities and were therefore unconstitutional.

This was a significant step forward, but it hardly put the matter to rest. On August 28, 1963, the Reverend Dr. Martin Luther King Jr. gave his famous "I have a dream" speech from the steps of the Lincoln Memorial in Washington, D.C. "I have a dream," he said, "that one day this nation will rise up and live out the true meaning of its creed: 'We hold these truths to be self-evident: that all men are created equal.'" That was almost a half century ago. Yet making Dr. King's dream come true, as well as erasing other injustices based on religion, gender, or sexual orientation, remains a challenge even today.

IT IS EASY TO TAKE THE DECLARATION of Independence for granted because its contents—which were revolutionary at the time—went on to become the foundation of our country's political philosophy. With the advantage of historical hindsight, we also know that the success of the American Revolution ensured that the way of life the colonists cherished would go on after the war ended.

Even though events turned out as the delegates had hoped, the outcome doesn't lessen the risks they shouldered. Had the war gone differently and the British restored their rule, many if not all of the delegates would have been arrested for treason. Their lands and possessions would have been forfeited to the Crown, and imprisonment or death would have been their likely fates. The possibility of execution was particularly riveting and painful, since under British law at the time traitors were partially hanged, disemboweled while still alive, and then beheaded.

So it is no small thing that colonial leaders were willing to take such chances. In 1776, when kings and queens, czars and emperors, maharajahs and shoguns ruled the world, the delegates of the Second Continental Congress were promoting an untested idea—that when an existing government does not properly serve its people, those people should dismiss that government and put a new one in its place. America's Founding Fathers did not see themselves as brave or heroic so much as respectable and honorable. They wished their deeds to be viewed as the actions of intelligent and reasonable men, reluctant patriots whom circumstances had forced to take extreme measures. In that light, and in their own minds, creating the Declaration of Independence was nothing more and nothing less than doing the right thing.

Once the Declaration was published, Congress had copies sent throughout the colonies, where its contents were proclaimed at large and small assemblies, to official political bodies and to the army. Always recognized for its historical significance, the original document was often on the move. After the creation of the United States in 1789, custody of the paper became the responsibility of the Department of State. In 1841 the Declaration was moved to the Patent Office, where it spent thirty-six years before returning to the State Department in 1877. By 1894, the document was clearly deteriorating, and it was withdrawn from public display. However, it was returned to view in the 1920s under the control of the Library of Congress. During World War II, it was temporarily moved for safekeeping to Fort Knox in Kentucky (where it shared quarters with billions of dollars in gold bullion). The National

The Declaration of Independence, on view for all to see in the rotunda of the
National Archives Building in Washington, D.C.

Archives took charge of the Declaration in 1952. Today, the original document, written on parchment, sits on display in the rotunda of the National Archives Building in Washington, D.C. It is protected by a specially constructed glass case filled with inert argon gas and a lot of computer technology that watches for any signs of further deterioration.

> *"I have never had a feeling politically that did not spring from the sentiments embodied in the Declaration of Independence."*
>
> —Abraham Lincoln

Thomas Jefferson would have been glad of that. Of all his many achievements and positions, he was proudest of one thing, which is why the epitaph on his tombstone begins, "Here was buried Thomas Jefferson, Author of the Declaration of American Independence."

As for the lasting benefit of the Declaration, President Abraham Lincoln perhaps best summed it up. Speaking on Washington's Birthday in 1861, Lincoln said, "I have never had a feeling politically that did not spring from the sentiments embodied in the Declaration of Independence." It was a document, he declared, that promoted the idea of "liberty, not alone to the people of this country, but, I hope to the world, for all future time."

The Declaration of Independence

FROM THE U.S. NATIONAL ARCHIVES &
RECORDS ADMINISTRATION

IN CONGRESS, July 4, 1776.

The unanimous Declaration of the thirteen united States of America,

When in the Course of human events, it becomes necessary for one people to dissolve the political bands which have connected them with another, and to assume among the powers of the earth, the separate and equal station to which the Laws of Nature and of Nature's God entitle them, a decent respect to the opinions of mankind requires that they should declare the causes which impel them to the separation.

We hold these truths to be self-evident, that all men are created equal, that they are endowed by their Creator with certain unalienable Rights, that among these are Life, Liberty and the pursuit of Happiness.—That to secure these rights, Governments are instituted among

Men, deriving their just powers from the consent of the governed,—That whenever any Form of Government becomes destructive of these ends, it is the Right of the People to alter or to abolish it, and to institute new Government, laying its foundation on such principles and organizing its powers in such form, as to them shall seem most likely to effect their Safety and Happiness. Prudence, indeed, will dictate that Governments long established should not be changed for light and transient causes; and accordingly all experience hath shewn, that mankind are more disposed to suffer, while evils are sufferable, than to right themselves by abolishing the forms to which they are accustomed. But when a long train of abuses and usurpations, pursuing invariably the same Object evinces a design to reduce them under absolute Despotism, it is their right, it is their duty, to throw off such Government, and to provide new Guards for their future security.—Such has been the patient sufferance of these Colonies; and such is now the necessity which constrains them to alter their former Systems of Government. The history of the present King of Great Britain is a history of repeated injuries and usurpations, all having in direct object the establishment of an absolute Tyranny over these States. To prove this, let Facts be submitted to a candid world.

He has refused his Assent to Laws, the most wholesome and necessary for the public good.

He has forbidden his Governors to pass Laws of immediate and pressing importance, unless suspended in their operation till his Assent should be obtained; and when so suspended, he has utterly neglected to attend to them.

He has refused to pass other Laws for the accommodation of large districts of people, unless those people would relinquish the right of Representation in the Legislature, a right inestimable to them and formidable to tyrants only.

He has called together legislative bodies at places unusual, uncomfortable, and distant from the depository of their public Records, for the sole purpose of fatiguing them into compliance with his measures.

He has dissolved Representative Houses repeatedly, for opposing with manly firmness his invasions on the rights of the people.

He has refused for a long time, after such dissolutions, to cause others to be elected; whereby the Legislative powers, incapable of Annihilation, have returned to the People at large for their exercise; the State remaining in the mean time exposed to all the dangers of invasion from without, and convulsions within.

He has endeavoured to prevent the population of these States; for that purpose obstructing the Laws for Naturalization of Foreigners; refusing to pass others to encourage their migrations hither, and raising the conditions of new Appropriations of Lands.

He has obstructed the Administration of Justice, by refusing his Assent to Laws for establishing Judiciary powers.

He has made Judges dependent on his Will alone, for the tenure of their offices, and the amount and payment of their salaries.

He has erected a multitude of New Offices, and sent hither swarms of Officers to harrass our people, and eat out their substance.

He has kept among us, in times of peace, Standing Armies without the Consent of our legislatures.

He has affected to render the Military independent of and superior to the Civil power.

He has combined with others to subject us to a jurisdiction foreign to our constitution, and unacknowledged by our laws; giving his Assent to their Acts of pretended Legislation:

For Quartering large bodies of armed troops among us:

For protecting them, by a mock Trial, from punishment for any Murders which they should commit on the Inhabitants of these States:

For cutting off our Trade with all parts of the world:

For imposing Taxes on us without our Consent:

For depriving us in many cases, of the benefits of Trial by Jury:

For transporting us beyond Seas to be tried for pretended offences:

For abolishing the free System of English Laws in a neighbouring Province, establishing therein an Arbitrary government, and enlarging its Boundaries so as to render it at once an example and fit instrument for introducing the same absolute rule into these Colonies:

For taking away our Charters, abolishing our most

valuable Laws, and altering fundamentally the Forms of our Governments:

For suspending our own Legislatures, and declaring themselves invested with power to legislate for us in all cases whatsoever.

He has abdicated Government here, by declaring us out of his Protection and waging War against us.

He has plundered our seas, ravaged our Coasts, burnt our towns, and destroyed the lives of our people.

He is at this time transporting large Armies of foreign Mercenaries to compleat the works of death, desolation and tyranny, already begun with circumstances of Cruelty & perfidy scarcely paralleled in the most barbarous ages, and totally unworthy the Head of a civilized nation.

He has constrained our fellow Citizens taken Captive on the high Seas to bear Arms against their Country, to become the executioners of their friends and Brethren, or to fall themselves by their Hands.

He has excited domestic insurrections amongst us, and has endeavoured to bring on the inhabitants of our frontiers, the merciless Indian Savages, whose known rule of warfare, is an undistinguished destruction of all ages, sexes and conditions.

In every stage of these Oppressions We have Petitioned for Redress in the most humble terms: Our repeated Petitions have been answered only by repeated injury. A Prince, whose character is thus marked by every act which may define a Tyrant, is unfit to be the ruler of a free people.

Nor have We been wanting in attentions to our Brittish brethren. We have warned them from time to time of attempts by their legislature to extend an unwarrantable jurisdiction over us. We have reminded them of the circumstances of our emigration and settlement here. We have appealed to their native justice and magnanimity, and we have conjured them by the ties of our common kindred to disavow these usurpations, which, would inevitably interrupt our connections and correspondence. They too have been deaf to the voice of justice and of consanguinity. We must, therefore, acquiesce in the necessity, which denounces our Separation, and hold them, as we hold the rest of mankind, Enemies in War, in Peace Friends.

We, therefore, the Representatives of the united States of America, in General Congress, Assembled, appealing to the Supreme Judge of the world for the rectitude of our intentions, do, in the Name, and by Authority of the good People of these Colonies, solemnly publish and declare, That these United Colonies are, and of Right ought to be Free and Independent States; that they are Absolved from all Allegiance to the British Crown, and that all political connection between them and the State of Great Britain, is and ought to be totally dissolved; and that as Free and Independent States, they have full Power to levy War, conclude Peace, contract Alliances, establish Commerce, and to do all other Acts and Things which Independent States may of right do. And for the support of this Declaration, with a firm reliance on the protection of divine Providence, we mutually pledge to each other our Lives, our Fortunes and our sacred Honor.

THE 56 SIGNATURES ON THE DECLARATION

GEORGIA:

Button Gwinnett

George Walton

Lyman Hall

NORTH CAROLINA:

William Hooper

John Penn

Joseph Hewes

SOUTH CAROLINA:

Edward Rutledge

Thomas Lynch, Jr.

Thomas Heyward, Jr.

Arthur Middleton

MASSACHUSETTS:

John Hancock

Samuel Adams

John Adams

Robert Treat Paine

Elbridge Gerry

NEW JERSEY:

Richard Stockton

John Witherspoon

Francis Hopkinson

John Hart

Abraham Clark

RHODE ISLAND:

Stephen Hopkins

William Ellery

VIRGINIA:

George Wythe

George Wythe

Th: Nelson jr.

Thomas Nelson, Jr.

Richard Henry Lee

Richard Henry Lee

Francis Lightfoot Lee

Francis Lightfoot Lee

Th Jefferson

Thomas Jefferson

Carter Braxton

Carter Braxton

Benj Harrison

Benjamin Harrison

PENNSYLVANIA:

Rob Morris

Robert Morris

Jas Smith

James Smith

Benjamin Rush

Benjamin Rush

Geo. Taylor

George Taylor

Benj. Franklin

Benjamin Franklin

James Wilson

James Wilson

John Morton

John Morton

Geo. Ross

George Ross

Geo Clymer

George Clymer

DELAWARE:

Caesar Rodney

Thomas McKean

George Read

NEW YORK:

William Floyd

Francis Lewis

Philip Livingston

Lewis Morris

CONNECTICUT:

Roger Sherman

William Williams

Samuel Huntington

Oliver Wolcott

MARYLAND:

Samuel Chase

Thomas Stone

William Paca

Charles Carroll of
Carrollton

NEW HAMPSHIRE:

Josiah Bartlett

Matthew Thornton

William Whipple

A CALL FOR LIBERTY

p. 7, "We must be unanimous . . .": A. J. Langguth,
Patriots: The Men Who Started the American Revolution
(New York: Simon and Schuster, 1988), 363.

p. 7, "We must all hang . . .": John Bartlett, *Bartlett's
Familiar Quotations,* 16th ed., edited by Justin
Kaplan (Boston: Little, Brown and Company,
1992), 310.

CHAPTER ONE: WELCOME TO THE NEW WORLD

p. 16, "the restoration of union . . .": W. C. Ford, ed.,
Journals of the Continental Congress (Washington,
DC: Library of Congress, 1904), 1:63.

p. 22, "I heard the bullets whistle . . .": Stephen Krensky,
George Washington: The Man Who Would Not Be King
(New York: Scholastic, 1991), 22.

p. 22, "leaped from his saddle . . .": David McCollough,
1776 (New York: Simon and Schuster, 2005), 61.

p. 24, "Some writers have so confounded . . .": Edward
Larkin, ed., *Common Sense by Thomas Paine*
(Peterborough, ON: Broadview Press, 2004), 46.

p. 25, "I have heard it asserted . . .": Ibid.

p. 27, "Great Britain has at last . . .": Frank Shuffelton,
ed., *The Letters of John and Abigail Adams* (New York:
Penguin Books, 2004), 172.

p. 27, "these United Colonies . . .": Hugh Chisholm, ed.,
The Encyclopaedia Britannica, 11th ed. (New York:

Encyclopaedia Britannica Company, 1911), 16:362.

p. 29, "The tree of liberty . . .": David C. Rapoport and Leonard Weinberg, eds., *The Democratic Experience and Political Violence* (Portland, OR: Frank Cass Publishers, 2001), 261.

p. 33, "Yesterday the greatest Question . . .": John Rhodehamel, ed., *The American Revolution: Writings from the War of Independence* (New York: Library of America, 2001), 125.

Chapter Two: A Formidable Juggling Act

p. 36, "Whether I had gathered my ideas . . .": Albert Ellery Bergh, ed., *The Writings of Thomas Jefferson* (Cambridge, MA: Harvard University Press, 1905), 462.

p. 36, "Neither aiming at originality . . .": Merrill Patterson, ed., *Thomas Jefferson* (New York: Library of America, 1984), 1501.

p. 37, "When in the Course . . .": Robert Maynard Hutchins, ed. in chief, *Great Books of the Western World* (Chicago: Encyclopaedia Britannica, 1952), 43:1.

p. 38, "all men are by nature. . .": Howard W. Preston, *Documents Illustrative of American History 1606-1863* (New York: G. P. Putnam's Sons, 1886), 206.

p. 40, "We hold these truths to be self-evident . . .": Ibid.

p. 41, "We hold these truths to be sacred ...": Robert Leckie, *George Washington's War: The Saga of the American Revolution* (New York: HarperCollins, 1992), 254.

p. 41, "among which are the preservation ...": Gunnar Myrdal, *An American Dilemma,* vol. 1, *The Negro Problem and Modern Democracy* (New York: HarperCollins, 1996), 9.

p. 41, "That to secure these rights ...": Robert Maynard Hutchins, ed. in chief, *Great Books of the Western World* (Chicago: Encyclopaedia Britannica, 1952), 43:1.

p. 44, "When a long train ...": Ibid.

p. 45, "history of repeated injuries ...": Ibid.

p. 46, "totally unworthy ...": Ibid.

p. 46, "In every stage ...": Ibid.

p. 47, "We have appealed ...": Ibid.

p. 47, "these United Colonies ...": Ibid.

p. 48, "waged cruel war ...": Paul Leicester Ford, ed., *The Writings of Thomas Jefferson,* vol. 2, *1776-1781* (New York: G. P. Putnam's Sons, 1893), 52.

p. 49, "determined to keep ...": Ibid., 53.

p. 51, "in complaisance to South Carolina ...": Merrill Patterson, ed., *Thomas Jefferson* (New York: Library of America, 1984), 18.

p. 52, "inherent & inalienable ...": Carl Lotus Becker, *The Declaration of Independence: A Study in the History of Political Ideas* (Ithaca, NY: Cornell University Library, 1992), 199.

p. 52, "And for the support . . .": John P. Foley, ed., *The Jeffersonian Cyclopedia: A Comprehensive Collection of the Views of Thomas Jefferson* (New York: Funk and Wagnalls, 1900), 971.

p. 52, "We might have been . . .": David McCullough, *John Adams* (New York: Simon and Schuster, 2001), 135.

CHAPTER THREE: THE NEWS TRAVELS FAR AND WIDE

p. 55, "Thirteen clocks . . .": Merrill Jensen, *The Founding of a Nation: A History of the American Revolution, 1763-1776* (New York: Oxford University Press, 1968), 33.

p. 55, "Games, Sports, Guns . . .": John Rhodehamel, ed., *The American Revolution: Writings from the War of Independence* (New York: Library of America, 2001), 127.

p. 56, "I am well aware . . .": Ibid.

p. 58, "So daring and desperate . . .": David McCollough, *1776* (New York: Simon and Schuster, 2005), 292.

p. 61, "Congress shall make . . .": Robert Maynard Hutchins, ed. in chief, *Great Books of the Western World* (Chicago: Encyclopaedia Britannica, 1952), 43:17.

p. 61, "of all political . . .": Bryan-Paul Frost and Jeffrey Sikkenga, eds., *History of American Political Thought* (Lanham, MD: Lexington Books, 2003), 69.

p. 65, "remember, all Men . . .": John Rhodehamel,

ed., *The American Revolution: Writings from the War of Independence* (New York: Library of America, 2001), 117.

p. 66, "When, in the course . . ." [Declaration of Sentiments, 1848]: Virginia Schomp, *American Voices from the Women's Movement* (New York: Marshall Cavendish, 2007), 43.

p. 67, "The costume of women . . .": Tobi Tobias, *Obsessed by Dress* (Boston: Beacon Press, 2000), 127.

p. 69, "Four score and . . .": John Bartlett, *Bartlett's Familiar Quotations*, 16th ed., edited by Justin Kaplan (Boston: Little, Brown and Company, 1992), 450.

p. 69, "Neither slavery nor . . .": Robert Maynard Hutchins, ed. in chief, *Great Books of the Western World* (Chicago: Encyclopaedia Britannica, 1952), 43:18.

p. 70, "I have a dream . . .": Martin Luther King Jr., *The Words of Martin Luther King, Jr.* (New York: Newmarket Press, 1996), 95.

CONCLUSION

p. 74, "I have never had . . .": Don E. Fehrenbacher, ed., *Lincoln, Speeches and Writings 1859–1865* (New York: Literary Classics of the United States, 1989), 213.

FOR FURTHER INFORMATION

BOOKS

Driver, Stephanie Schwartz. *The Declaration of Independence.* Hauppauge, NY: Barrons, 2004.

Freedman, Russell. *Give Me Liberty: The Story of the Declaration of Independence.* New York: Holiday House, 2002.

Hakim, Joy. *A History of US.* Vol. 3, *From Colonies to Country 1735-1791.* New York: Oxford University Press, 2007.

Sheinkin, Steve. *King George: What Was His Problem?* New York: Roaring Brook, 2008.

WEBSITES

Declaration of Independence: Thomas Jefferson (Library of Congress Exhibition)
www.loc.gov/exhibits/jefferson/jeffdec.html
This Library of Congress site features material on Thomas Jefferson, particularly during the time he was writing the Declaration of Independence.

Declaration of Independence
www.archives.gov/exhibits/charters/declaration.html
The U.S. Government Archives feature a close-up look at the Declaration.

Interactive John Trumbull's "Declaration of Independence"
www.quiz-tree.com/Declaration-of-Independence-Trumbull.html

This site displays John Trumbull's famous painting of the presentation of the Declaration to Congress, which Trumbull painted after consulting with Thomas Jefferson and meeting many of the other signers. Visitors can identify and learn more about the participants by dragging the mouse across the image.

SELECTED BIBLIOGRAPHY

The Declaration of Independence. In Hutchins, Robert Maynard, ed. in chief. *Great Books of the Western World*. Vol. 43. Chicago: Encyclopaedia Britannica, 1952.

Bailyn, Bernard. *The Ideological Origins of the American Revolution*. Cambridge, MA: Harvard University Press, 1967.

Becker, Carl. *The Declaration of Independence: A Study in the History of Political Ideas*. New York: Vantage Books, 1922.

Bober, Natalie S. *Countdown to Independence: A Revolution of Ideas in England and Her American Colonies*. New York: Atheneum Books for Young Readers, 2001.

Donovan, Frank. *Mr. Jefferson's Declaration: The Story behind the Declaration of Independence*. New York: Dodd, Mead and Company, 1968.

Fischer, David Hackett. *Washington's Crossing*. New York: Oxford University Press, 2004.

McCullough, David. *1776*. New York: Simon and Schuster, 2005.

Rhodehamel, John, ed. *The American Revolution: Writings from the War of Independence*. New York: Library of America, 2001.

Wood, Gordon. *Revolutionary Characters: What Made the Founders Different*. New York: Penguin Press, 2006.

INDEX

Hutchinson, Thomas, 64

Intolerable Acts, 14

Jefferson, Thomas, **6**, 19
  and Declaration of Inde-
    pendence, 28–29, 30, **31**,
    34, 35–46, 74
  and slavery, 48, 49, 51

King, Martin Luther Jr.,
  69–70

Lee, Arthur, 60
Lee Resolution, 27–28, 30
Lee, Richard Henry, 27, 60
Lexington and Concord,
  Battle of, 16–17, **17**, 20
Lincoln, Abraham, 68–69, 74
Livingston, Robert R., 28
Locke, John, 36, 42–44, **42**
Louis XVI (France), 63

Madison, James, 19
Maryland, 28
Mason, George, 38
Massachusetts, 10, 22, 26,
  28, 64
Morris, Robert, 58
Mott, Lucretia, 66

Navigation Acts, 14
New Jersey, 28
New World, American
  colonists in, 9–16
New York, 28, 32
North Carolina, 26

Paine, Thomas, 23, 24–26, **24**
Pennsylvania, 9, 10, 28, 32
Philadelphia, **8**, 16, 29–30, **29**
Plessy v. Ferguson, 69
Puritans, 10

Quakers, 10, **10**

racial and gender equality
  issues, 64–68, **65**, **67**
Randolph, Peyton, 19
Revere, Paul, 16
Rockingham, Marquis of,
  58–59

Second Continental Con-
  gress, 6, **6**, 16–17, 18–19,
  18, 20, 36, 71–72
Sherman, Roger, 28
slavery, 48–51, **50**, 64, 68–70
Sons of Liberty, 15
South Carolina, 26, 49, 51
Stamp Act, 14

ABOUT THE AUTHOR

STEPHEN KRENSKY is the author of more than one hundred fiction and nonfiction books for children, including many about American history. He has written chapter-book biographies of Barack Obama, Benjamin Franklin, and George Washington as well as shorter works on the Salem witch trials, Paul Revere, John Adams, the California gold rush, George Washington Carver, Annie Oakley, and the Wright Brothers.